Lullaby of Love

Selected Poems

Rebecca Winning

Indian Paintbrush Poets

Colorado

Copyright © 2025 by Rebecca Winning

Second Edition

All rights reserved. Printed in the United States of America. No part of this book may be used or reproduced in any manner whatsoever without written permission except in the case of brief quotations embodied in written articles and reviews. For information contact:

Pearn and Associates, Inc.
3518 Kingston Circle
Fort Collins, CO 80525
Publishing Books People Love Reading

Cover Design
Megan Ryan

Published by
Indian Paintbrush Poets
An imprint of Pearn and Associates, Inc.
A Veteran Owned Company

Library of Congress Catalog Number 2025936885

ISBN: 978-1-7357731-3-1

*For Jim and Mary Winning
who modeled enduring love
and Jack Gill
who helps me live it every day*

Acknowledgements

Grateful acknowledgement is made to the following:

Ball State University Forum, for "Sister"
Alchemist Review, for "Fifth Street Blind Man" and
    "Strangers"
Portfolio, for "In Late Morning"
Mississippi Valley Review, for "Last Letter"
Kansas Quarterly, for "Sometimes"
Spoon River Quarterly, for "The Other Woman"
Tiny Moments, for "Intention"
Illinois Times, for "Cure for Backache"
Sangamon Poets, Sangamon State University,
    Springfield, Illinois, for
    Cure for Backache and Other Poems
Moonsquilt Press, for
    A Marriage Pact and Other Poems

Special thanks to Victor Pearn, president of Pearn and Associates Inc., who inspires me with his dedication to poetry every day.

Contents

Early Poems 1

Sister 3
Fifth Street Blind Man 4
For J 5
In Late Morning 6
In a Moment of Stone 7
Last Letter 8
Letter to Linda 10

From A Cure for Backache and Other Poems, 1977 13

Fall Housecleaning 15
Waiting 16
Another Day 17
The Woman in the Mirror 18
Cure for Backache 19
Backpacking, 1975 20
Grandmother 21
Picture a House 22

From A Marriage Pact and Other Poems, 1983 23

A Marriage Pact 25
At Night 27
Strangers 28
Sometimes 30
Bedtime 31
The Word Marriage 32
Early Morning 33
The Other Woman 34
Falsifying the Record 35
Landscape 36
Holding On 37
Paper, Rock, Scissors 38
Pursuing Your Skin 40

Child   41
Water Witch   42
Woman to Man   43

The Middle Years   45

Babbling   47
Starlings   49
Bringing in Firewood   50
Park / April   52
Sooner or Later   53
Light Rain, Summer   55
Christmas, Washington Park   57
When the Rain Has Forgotten You   58
Untitled   59
The Grass Parts to Receive You   60
Rain Coming   61
My Grandmother's Piano   62
Landscape   63
UFO   64
Believing in Magic   65
Farther Out   66

New Poems   67

2020 Burning   69
Intention   71
High Wind Warning   72
Caving   73
Vigil   75
Grandchild   77
Late April   78
Leaving   79
To Be Set Adrift   80

Early Poems

Sister

Each visit a celebration: we window shop,
drink tea, repot some plants, and
flip through magazines. The sun softens
your kitchen with its last light.
We boil spaghetti and David
goes out for L'Ambrusco.
Your life's too settled to be simple.

Secretly, I glean the air for friction,
thinking, *"How can she be happy?*
Where did she decide, and how?" though
on your couch I learn a dreamless sleep,
and when the window yawns to a morning
all mystical and chaste,
even I awaken into grace.

I feel allied with symmetry, in balance
with the past. We talk of family,
old Christmases, the games we played on Bates.
We giggle like teenagers. We choose names
for the children you are going to have.
I am in love with this respectable love.
Vermeer should have painted you.

I stir and stir my tea,
watching the morning moving into place, till,
nudged by a shoulder of sun, I rise to go.
Dark seeds are in my hand, and I
must plant my own garden
                        I take one look back
to see you, wearing your yellow sunhat,
your arms full of forsythia.

Fifth Street Blind Man

Things become known through a shudder
in the flesh. I hear the swish

of corduroy — nylons sliding
through the light litter of wind —

the thresh of thigh on thigh
filling the air. *Whose soft skirt is swinging?*

Whose hair? I am surrounded
by an ebb and flow of sound,

barbed with scents of make-up,
of perfume: little hooks that snag the skin

and whisper through the network of my nerves:
I'm here. I have something to say.

I lean back. I wait. I listen —
to distance — things moving away.

For J

Put it in my pocket,
it jangles like a set of keys.

On a table,
it refracts the light,
splits the celebration into showers.

I may hide it in my pillow;
it glimmers past my eyelids into dreams.
Drop it,
and its filamented rays will lead it home.

Shake hands with me.
See how intricate and light

this love, this dazzling Christmas penny
in my hand.

In Late Morning

In late morning
with the wick of sun turned up
and burning brightest, streams have eyes.
Branches and their shadows serve as hair.

Narcissus,
when the birdsong overhead
ran in honeyed notes along the river
changing the expression of the ripples

were you blind?
To have only seen yourself
among the hundreds? We cry, Narcissus,
and a thousand faces watch us from our tears.

In a Moment of Stone

In a moment of stone
the light falls sharp:
a line of shadow,
a closed silence.
There is more here
than I remember.

My face is blank
as the sky, turning away
from the patterns
of stars or birds.
My eyes are petrified,
white stones
in a white skull.

I am always on the edge
of something. I remember
a sense of birds
and their shadows; I feel
a kind of fluttering
warming the hollows
of my blood . . .

suggestions of rain,
a rustle of things
stirring . . . always at the edge.
When I turn to listen
the sound falls away.

So I sit: calm,
motionless, like a stone.
At my mind's edge
there is almost a picture:
the shell chipping away
revealing the bird.

Last Letter

Remember the day you
saddled your mares,
took me idling along beanfields,
the drone of insects
weaving the warp of air . . . .

Dust grew in the rows,
flowering up over hooves
and blossomed deadly and dry.
Not a cloud boiled up to break
the tension of that sky.

Then cicadas fell silent at a sting
of wind. Land listened
and bean plants turned up
the pale palms of their hands.
Rain eclipsed the horizon,

horses snorted and stirred
at a sudden scent of earth.
Turning them hard,
we raced the thundering rain
all the way back to the barn.

We closed the curtains
of your house, listened
to the wind whining at your door —
talked in quiet tones
lying on the floor.

I stared at you
the way a child stares
who is first beginning to see.
Under the cover of thrumming rain
you did not reach for me.

We lay there in silence,
my heart beating close to my bones.
You tucked a strand of hair behind
my ear, but did not smile.
I left before your wife got home.

Now rain freshens the night
And eight years gone.
I have met the man I will marry.
Tonight, he sleeps — his breath
a moth that flutters in the room.

I know now. We make our own weather:
surprise of sun, desire
that falls and rises like dark rain.
We make our own cycles of sorrow.
I will not write you again.

Letter to Linda
For Straz

Stars blurred to blue that morning.
We shivered into jeans
and started the long walk to town.

Wind shirred the trees.
We felt our way
along a rutted road.

Then morning swept the sky
and flowers appeared in the fields
as if the stars had fallen.

Houses huddled in sleep;
dreams curled up like smoke.
The swings in the spielplatz hung limp

awaiting a form. Enticed by bakery lights
we splurged
and bought a loaf of bread — still warm.

And the air was a swelling of scent,
a yeasty rising, gluten, like joy
ballooning and filling the heart —

butter a yellow rivering
and bread melting to nothing
in that German morning.

We did not talk about men.
Instead, we ate warm bread
and listened to the bright applause of birds.

Ten years have hardened the crusts
that hide the separate textures of our lives.
We have married and moved on.

We have both met the Other Woman
whose casual, red nails puncture the heart.
We have stood at our separate windows

watching the slow rise of snow
wondering, *What have I done?* and
Where did it all go?

Now I feel the chill of empty chairs.
My kitchen hides from the sun.
On days like this, I see us sitting there

and realize that friendships need not fail.
I will be fed. And life will go on rising —
that good bread.

*From A Cure For Backache
And Other Poems, 1977*

Fall Housecleaning

I swept you out with a vengeance
and let new sunlight fly around the rooms.

I vacuumed the smallest corners
snatching up the echoes of our conversations . . .

practiced smiling in the bathroom mirror,
thinking, "There, that's out of my life."

But I wasn't happy with that.

Then I found your kazoo behind the bookcase.
I pounced on it, delighted, like a cat.

I smoked it like a pipe,
played with it in the bathtub,

slept with it under my pillow
and used it to scratch my back.

Finally, I swallowed it whole.

Now the edges have gone out of my voice.
When I laugh, the sound is musical —

breathing brings the whispers
of strange comfort, and I look forward

to calling you up from some new city,
hearing about your kids, the years of your life,

sending my songs, my thanks.

Waiting

for the mirror to shatter, leaving one speck of silver,
for suns to rise out of my mouth, that the birds can
nest with and bless,
for my fingers to learn the kindness of petals,
for the hymen to stop renewing itself,

for the window shade of the soul to fly open,
for the light to come in
and go out again.

Another Day

This bald morning
is full of light and air.
Garbage men rattle the cans;
they have deep voices.
There is a clock
ticking its heart out.

The sun pours through
the windows, follows
the floorboards and
settles among the plants.
They turn to it
fully and slowly.

The Woman in the Mirror

When birds fly out of the landscape
it is for her.
Her hands cause the stones to open.
She absorbs sounds like light;
she is a silence.

The air blossoms in sunlight around her;
she has found stars in the caves of the earth.

Her patience begins to surround me.

She waits where I have been,
where I have always been going.

Cure for Backache

Imagine your wooden floors
are returning to trees;
your bedroom is filled with them.

Lie down among them.
Feel things growing in the earth
beneath you.

Pretend that you have never driven a car,
or smoked a cigarette. Breathe.
Allow your soul to become still.

Rearrange some historical event:
think of a tall Napoleon who played the fiddle
and wore sneakers; imagine

that we never closed off the rivers of Idaho,
invented the razor,
or stood for the testing of nuclear warheads.

Focus on something simple:
perhaps a trellis of morning glories,
or a wide porch with two wicker chairs.

Your hands will begin to feel heavy.
Smell them. Your right hand
will smell like the earth,

your left hand
will smell like the moon.
Now, walk out into the day.

Backpacking, 1975

We move into the heave and thrall
of the woodlands; leaves begin
to burn in autumn air. We go deeper
into thirst, the dark bruise of the hip strap;
the encouragement we take from one another.
Birds flutter up in the wind.
Spiders lace up the trails behind us.

We stop at last and cook our soup.
Tonight, I ask to wash the dishes;
you walk with me to the stream.
Night brings a falling of forest sounds,
a leafy breathing. Our darknesses
merge in one circle of light.
You play soft songs on your harmonica.

Grandmother
for Grace

In the sun, bringing in chrysanthemums.
Her hair silvers like the backs of maples.
She blinks and draws the circles
of her children's faces in the warm air:

one who has died in San Francisco,
one who collects books and paintings in New York,
one who builds dams and highways,
one who is like her, tending autumn flowers
under the arc of a Midwest sunset.

A chorus of laughter

> *a pocketful of posies*
> *ashes, ashes . . .*

                                      down the long afternoon.

There is light all around her.
She could dance in this percussion
of orange and yellow!

She gathers the flowers with an old hand.

Picture a House

There is an oak tree, so old,
two people holding hands
can't reach around it.

The house knows a quiet music,
in and out of the eves, over the kettle,
along the wooden floors . . .

There is room for breathing deeply,
for exhalations. A wide porch
shelters a garden of white begonias.

The kitchen is huge and filled with sun.
Cupboards are belly-full of home cannings;
the icebox is stocked with milk and cheese.

Whatever sorrows fall
are planted in the ground,
They bear good fruit.

There is a chair next to the window
where one can listen to rain;
drink the sound of lost summer
and lose the day's dust.

No one lives here,
yet.
The door is waiting to swing open.

*From A Marriage Pact
And Other Poems, 1983*

A Marriage Pact

We have begun now —
dark mornings with
snow drifting down, noon's
when sidewalks refuse it

rising like islands
through white. And evenings —
the yellow lamplight
that softens everything.

I have brought you
my hands, my silences . . .
my voice, that holds your name
deep in the throat.

What hums in my veins
is a private landscape —
birds skimming the skull
then coming to roost

in the fusty nest of the heart.
And loneliness, silently
prowling around these bones.
I keep wanting to curl up —

to sleep at the base of the brain
and dream the old stories.
The glass slipper. The enchanted
kiss. Always, there is the struggle

against that sleep. And you?
You're in another room,
drinking coffee; thinking, perhaps,
of silences, of human endurances —

a man in the deep hush of trees,
a man leaving footprints in snow.
I do not know your stories.
It is enough to think of you

dreaming, your hand asleep
in my hair . . . . Quietly,
your name floats
down the long hallway.

At Night

My hands dream. They touch you
in silence. It's as if
they were not really touching,
not trying to learn anything.
The whorls of my fingers
stumble on pebbles of sweat
and follow for hours
the long paths of your arms —
gliding through meadows, or climbing
into the rough. It is not enough.

They become birds —
skimming the twilight of your spine
to coo at the nape of your neck.
They soar into dreams
where leaves flare up
and breathe in whispers.
Secrets. Secrets.
Shapes pass by underneath,
Women. Water. Words.
It is not enough.

They become fish, moving
through shadows of blood,
moving against the tide,
squeezing through chambers
of your heart — moving;
wanting to spawn,
wanting to leave
something; caught in the pull
of blood rushing between dull
thuds of the heart . . . .

Light brings them back to my arms.
They greet the morning; they become hands.
They remember nothing.

Strangers

A sighing through screens
   — the leaves whisper —
and rain. The streets darken.

In another city, your mother
   is lost in sleep.
They can't say whether she dreams,

Among her things, we found a note
   from someone I never knew:
"Mommy, I love you." Perhaps

she dreams of you, wading home
   through waves of Kansas wheat
bringing a stringer of bullheads.

I hear her voice in the
   breathing dark.
Woman blood. Earth scents. Shadows.

I feel closer to her than to you —
   when you come in,
heavy and sorrowful — the world

reduced in your eyes.
   I am the china doll
you won at some carnival

though you can't seem to remember
   how, or even why.
I am as helpless as she is.

No gesture touches this rain —
   this long night, the heart
that will not be still, that keeps on

beating — frail, blind bird
   caught in a slow
contraction, expansion of bone.

We are all caught. It's as if
   we are in her dream.
I begin to love you like a son.

When you first come in,
   bent over against the rain,
I want to call out the name of your father.

Sometimes

Sometimes you leave me
for days. A shoe, an old
bread wrapper — something
swallows your voice.
You stare out a window
and go into a dream
that has no doorway.

I do not own you or know you.
I have felt the weight
of your hand asleep on my thigh.
What I have is the memory
of that hand. And fear,
pressing in with her moon face
at every window.

Sometimes, I am afraid
of disappearing.
The trees could gather me in —
a torch laugh cooled by leaves,
my words dissolved in small,
soft murmurings of birds.
The cold stars!

My hair floating,
my bones undone by wind . . . .
Do not leave me for long.
Sometimes it is hard —
this waiting —
for you to open the door
and call out my name.

Bedtime

I move in a sorrow of sorts;
there are dreams growing smaller
in my hand. There is nowhere to go
but here, and so I come
bringing more than you know.

The things that memory lights on:
long avenues of sunlight;
the green, arching trees; a laugh
that falters and runs on . . .
and more, even than these.

And where are you but here?
Falling forward from the boy you were.
The Kansas sky, the summer nights you've known
are all thinning out into distance; into a loneliness
that cannot be outgrown.

But there is comfort here,
in the way the sheets grow warm;
in the way you trace the outline
of my arm; in small talk
of the garden, of the weather.

We learn to dream by lying here
together. Love, I would give you
everything I keep —
light words to fill the darkness
till we sleep.

The Word Marriage

At first, I dreamed of weddings
that turned into trials. You were the defendant,
or I was — my father, the judge. Or else
I had the bride part in a play,
stood in the wings, itching, in white
to discover I'd learned the wrong lines.
Ordinary mornings found me
standing in the kitchen, cooking eggs.

I look at pictures of the two of us —
stephanotis, baby's breath —
and try the word. Husband.
It is a foreign language, born in the hills
where voices lilt, crazy with loneliness,
and there are many words for snow.
Someone bends over a café table:
"Are you hungry?"

Not the appropriate word.
I am tired of reading the signs
that direct our lives; I want to
meet with you in some pure space
where there is no language —
just the wild cry of paired birds
piercing the eye of distance
with the dark thread of their shadows.

Early Morning

Birds are waking in the pyracantha.
Orange berries and noise!
It is too much for a heart
grown suddenly small.

I don't know if you love me.

I come to wander here
in first bravura of morning
where daylight dizzies down
the narrow limbs of trees

to splinter on the thickened ice
and swans circle a shrinking pond
as if they were dreaming,
keeping it open.

You wander secret fields
lost in the leaves of sleep
afraid of eyes that blink
and disappear . . .

and I'm right here.

Longing opens the heart
and takes root in the forest of my bones.
I try, through splintered shards of light
to move, to keep a place that is my own.

The Other Woman

She explains everything.

The song that beat in your heart
is played out in the trembling
of your hands, and the slow turn
of the years stops here —
fixed forever in this bar, this hour,
the tiny paring of light
glinting red in your glass.

Outside, your footsteps echo on cement.
The moon is bloated with snow.
You are surprised to find the night,
the casual crowds, doing business
as usual. They do not notice
as your dreams go spinning away,
reduced to something small and hard —

a handful of ice crystals
caught in a tunnel of wind
and blown past lighted windows.

Falsifying the Record

It never snowed in summer.
The dogs that lunged at the door
were friendly and wagged their tails,
and love was not a snake
coiling tighter and tighter
around our ribs before
it slipped through our fingers.

This part is true:
cutworms invaded the garden,
a shocking green.
We picked them off when we saw them.
We dusted. We harvested.
And watched the slow ravage of leaves
all summer long.

Love was a blizzard in my head.
Love, for you, was a wave
that was always receding.
We were never prepared
for the weather; no one to blame.
We were, both of us,
innocent.

Landscape

A rush of color
and water swallows the sun.
Mayflies feed on the last
low glitters of light.

It is easy to think
of better times when
the raw cry of gulls
gets lost in the clouds

and their shadows go skipping
over the waves.
The red seam of sky
giving way. The marsh grass

shirring the darkness.
Easy to think of you
pushing me into bed
again and again

or your face blossoming
when I waved to you on the street.
I sat in a chair, waiting,
hidden by white curtains —

for the sound of your step
on the stair . . .
We must not argue.
On the table

a bowl of cold radishes,
and out past the darkened trees,
the water — calling us
over and over.

Holding On

Always in your pocket
there is a stone.
How it fascinates the fingers of one hand!
While the one is off, inclined to dance,
to revel in the leafy sky of words,
the other holds the stone,
poking a finger over and over
into each worn depression.

Things could be so sweet —
the tender curl of leaves,
a slice of cantaloupe —
with one hand to follow the flight of birds,
another to trace the curve
of someone's face . . . .

But one hand is always missing,
examining the weight
and texture of that stone.
A moon breaks loose
and floats up past the window;
twilight creeps in and deepens
and you think, *without this weight
I'd be flying*, ten fingers
combing the wind.
The insect sting of the stars!

You empty your pockets.
Gifts for everybody —
handkerchief, money, keys,
the pocketknife you've had since you were ten,
the buckeye you carry for luck –
everything!

Except for the stone.

Rock, Paper, Scissors

Paper.
That label on the tin can
of the world! That landscape!
The colors abundant and the salt
tapdancing on your tongue.
The fishes quick in your eye
except for the whales
that go lolling . . . .
Paper wraps rock.

Rock.
A stone of sorrow, sinking
through the waters
of your heart.
Birds drop to the ground
dead.
You wonder,
where does it come from?
Slowly, calmly,
as routine as the moon —
steadily sinking.
Rock crushes scissors.

Scissors.
The clean bite,
a delicate steel; it is a way
to narrow things down.
You call it love with its sharp edges.
You want to shine!
You want someone to *use* you.
Scissors cut paper.

Paper wraps rock.
Again!
You have never been fond of games;
they're so stupid,
so tiresome.
You keep wanting to wield your scissors
against your stone.

But what can you do?
There are children in this house.
The long minutes go stuttering on;
the odds are neither for you
nor against you, and suddenly,
the evening has you surrounded.

You might as well go on playing.

Pursuing Your Skin

You know it is out there somewhere,
the one that precisely fits —
where you can sense patterns
of light and shadow, playing
across your shoulders, or feel wind
teasing your fingers. You have
glimpsed it at night
wading the river of moon that weaves
through the trees, or mornings,
when it rises from sleep
while you're still dreaming.
You wonder where it goes in the daylight.

You hear a sigh in an empty bedroom,
or a low, soft song from the bath,
You can imagine slipping it on
— finger by finger, toe by toe —
silken, unwrinkled.
You think of making love in such a skin,
a hand brushing your thigh,
belly, nest, the bright sheen of new sweat.
You think it must hunger for substance,
and wonder why it eludes you
at the end of the long day
when you walk down the echoing hallway.

Child

Not mine. Not mine.
Swelling of the seasons
leaves me dry.
Hidden voices in the leaves
hush
when I go by.

A child cries
in my mind; the thin sound
floats through my bones.
Someone brown-haired
and brown-eyed
is trying to find
her way home.

Somewhere cells will split
in celebration —
   gill
      finger
          ear —
A heart will start to echo
in the deep

for some other woman to hear
for some other woman to keep.

Water Witch

A woman moves in a grove of trees
in and out of shadow. She is serene
as a Vermeer; the harsh light
cannot harm her.

She strips a branch down to white bone
in a dry bed of river. Untouched
by heat or drought, she can remember
the sound of water.

The earth tugs at her arms, her heart —
the trees above her shudder. In her womb
she feels the rhythmic pull of nursing
a child or a lover.

Woman to Man

There are days when sun tinges the trees
and leaves come lazying down
against a measure of pure blue
and I feel like reaching up small hands.
But there are days when hands close —
when they shutter themselves, finger by finger
to shelter a mess of shadows — days
when I am not sure of what I know.

Then, I cannot reach out to you,
or enter your strange rooms of silence
walled in by vertical light.
Sometimes I need a totally open space —
an endless field – where darkness can bend down
and scatter like shadows in bright grass;
where hawks float quietly overhead
spiraling into the distance.

Sometimes I need the woman that is in you.

She will say yes. She will plant a meadow
of light words. Against a deepening evening,
she will turn to me and say,
"What do you have hidden in your hands?"
And knowing how hard it can be
to believe that such miracles happen
she will wait for the light to bloom in them
when petal by petal, they open.

The Middle Years

Babbling

No one understands me.
I speak of joy —
simple, connected,
rooted like grass,
growing out of the air,
then walking off into sunlight:
madman, magician, idiot.

I see you in an alley.
You are leaning against a doorjamb
like a modern-day James Dean.
You are smoking a cigarette and
waiting for something to happen.

Listen. I don't want
anything. Only to say
I have seen the squares
where pigeons change from light
to dark and back to light again
like two-sided coins, turning
and turning in sunlight.

I am dancing down to you
banging garbage can lids,
pointing out geraniums in clay pots
that bloom in this twilight of dust.

I'm here, I tell you
in my unintelligible tongue.
I jump up and down,
pick a geranium and plant
its small explosion
behind my ear.
I make a fool of myself, laughing —

waiting for you to turn
away from the shadows, so that light
can come into your eyes.

Starlings

You loved / love him
so much!

You say he bedded you
the night before he came
to marry me.
And after.

For a while I watched the birds
dragging the muddy clouds.
Stars came floating up.
Sunrise bloodied the waters.

I loved him too.
I was so sad.

Now it is colder;
the wild geese have flown on.
I no longer dream
about death.

We are all blind men.
We poke our sticks
into bushes
until the last leaf falls.

What I mean is this:
I forgive myself.
I put the stick away.

It's late in the year
and the starlings are starting to gather.

Bringing in Firewood

The wind over the river.
The sad quena of trees.

Snow — a slow, white sigh
that muffles the garden.

The yard fills up with dark.
I am out here

looking for miracles.
A world waits to be born:

buds cuddled up,
cicadas sucking roots,

small frogs huddled in mud.
I wonder whether they dream?

Now — while pale lungs
wither and bloom

slower than snow,
slower than morning

that waits at the mouth of the river
to swallow the dark —

do eyes twitch,
seeing lush leaves,

the river ringing with water
rushing past shocks of wild roses?

The cold is incandescent,
burning my bare hands.

Clouds escape from my lungs
and rise, as if asking a question . . . .

Will lilies spear the inertia of August?
Will the wrens come back?

Will we go on loving each other?
I am bringing in wood

while you wait by the fire —
green peppers hot in the oven

and thick mugs brimming with milk.
Snow dizzies down

in a hush of relentless joy
as after carols, or bells.

My footprints will go under.
No one will know where I stood.

But I, in the middle of summer —
when cicadas cut the heat

with the sound of saws
and frogs call over the water

will remember the light and the wonder
of loving you, bringing in wood.

Park / April

Trees are taut
with the tension between sound bark
and white, inner wood —
light trapped in a tight binding.
See how it all spills over into leaves,
all shining!

Small children
call out among shadows
as they race one another
along a long line of birches.
Fast as they are, they can't keep up
with their voices.

Sooner or Later

Sooner or later, love will sneak into your house.
As when, in autumn, the smoke of twilight rises up,
goes cold, and skitters down
in tiny grains of snow between the weeds
and mice slip in through chinks in brick
blinking at the artificial light.

You don't even know that they're there.

And then some evening, as you're humming —
tossing clams into cioppino
and hunting in the pantry
for a hunk of bread, you find
scattered droppings littering the shelves.
Later, when you entertain, you see
a quick, black shadow dart along the wall.

You smile sweetly, pretending it didn't happen.

Then morning, in the upstairs room
the window lightens to a square of gray
and you lie in the pocket of warmth
you make between the sheets, hushed, and drowsy,
and still, and suddenly, you are startled into the day
by a mad, scrambling panic in the walls.

You think of setting traps behind the stove
but you cannot bear to hear
the telling snap of capture, or to dream
of bleaching bones, scattered
in the desert of your sleep.

Finally, it surprises you.
One day you reach for a book
and find it peering down from the bookshelf,

its whiskers quivering, its black eyes
bright as beaded ink. You see the tiny paws
pressed into its chest, trembling
with the hammering of its heart.

Your own heart squeaks with fear
And a tiny pain . . . .

     Sooner or later,
love will sneak into your house.
And what will you do with it?
Where will it go? — as you go on,
waiting for summer.

Light Rain, Summer

What is there to be sad about
in the evening, when you go walking?

It rains, and the sun is still shining.
The fragrance of summer is rising

while little pins of light go slanting
into the grass. So. Why is it sad?

The rain leaves tiny pawprints on the lake.
The ducks go right on sailing in slow circles.

Rain pats the back of your shadow
there, on the ground, and *that*

is what you feel: the light of the rain
on your shadow and not the real rain.

Not the real you. You feel
the endless possibilities that could move

in any direction: your shadow
stretched out on the grass

and cold light sinking into it.
Your heart fills up with water.

Your heart grows heavy
and buries itself in the grass.

There is no reason for this!
You take hold of your sorrow

as if you were leading a child
and walk out of the park

past the long rows of apartments.
Rain follows you into the city.

When you think of this
you will remember the blazing light

falling quickly into the leaves;
how they trembled, how beautiful it was.

Christmas, Washington Park

On this clear night
even the snow is sharp-
edged, shivering down
through the trees.
Your footsteps grow quiet.
Quiet.
      The wind quickens
and you can almost hear
the tiny, chiming crystals
collide in the dark.

You can remember
cottonwood, foaming
over the curbstones,
stumbling like whitecaps
over the waves of grass —
how it floated, luminous and soft
over the noise of the playground.

Now it is silent.
It is all so innocent.

Always, the whisper of memory
drifting down through the days
and always a voice telling stories:
What if, what if . . . .

It is hard to tell the one
from the other.

Even now,
in the deep hush of winter
the clamorous white birds
are rising up from your heart
to soar out over the water.

When the Rain Has Forgotten You . . . .

You can picture the tender grass
growing out of your skull,
roots reaching under your tongue
and your teeth yielding . . . .

When the rain stops, everything listens.

Out front, the street is deserted:
dark houses harboring dreams
in whirling currents of sleep;
the blurred circles of streetlights
floating, green, in the leaves.

Out back there are shimmering trees,
black fingers tangled in hair
shaking out water and stars,
and the drip of left-over rain
splattering onto the patio.

One wants not to be forgotten.

One wants, always, to live by other lights:
the lopsided moon, washed clean —
the line of streetlights, striding off
boldly, into the dark.

Untitled

Just before morning,
before the first bird
lilts into the world's sleep
to let in an almond light,
that's the time
when I am most myself.

Or later, when twilight
begins to loosen
the alveoli of leaves;
when trees begin breathing
and winds put the moon
into motion — I soften.

My outlines blend into shadows;
I move in the moving air —
when the world stands, slightly
off center, fully at home
in the light that is both
there and not there.

The Grass Parts to Receive You . . . .

A waste of time
to be always
thinking and thinking
how you fit
into the world.

Tempting!
But useless.

The grass parts
to receive you
and short, hot winds
go pushing
at your back.

You think how the ground
will cover you —
packed down by careless
feet; your hair
gone dry as straw
and no one to repeat
the precise
lilt
of your voice.

Thinking and thinking
you are liable to miss
the other, singing
voices.

Rain Coming . . . .

After the long summer
clouds tumble down
heavy with brash light —
thunder.

In this rocker
I sit absolutely still.
Plants hang in corners of quiet;
shadows are draped over chairs.

All season I have learned to wait —
to wait and shelter a happiness
small and dry as a walnut.
I keep my hands in my lap,
two white sleeping birds.

Now, wind bullies the bushes
and shouts out a cold
regenerative curse.
My white face stares back
from the window —

behind the eyes,
pure water, and birds
diving into green trees.

My Grandmother's Piano

Late afternoons. The old upright —
that keeper of keys,
that dark mountain of sound.
If you pushed the pedals
you got storms!

I would polish and polish
legs that looked like claws.
I wanted to go into the echo,
that place where the water was,
and sunlight all bright on the river,
and the troll's
terrible
voice.

I poked holes in all the black paper
lining the ornate carve-outs
in the box above the keyboard;
waited to catch the music pouring out,
but inside were only wires
and little green hammers
that plunked down.

My mother came in with a dark face,
but then she smiled.
She looked like the sun.
We did chopsticks at least ten times.

Big hands, little hands,
playing.

Landscape

Spring has come to loosen my bones.
My lungs breathe freely as leaves.

The skeletons
that stalked the horizon
take on flesh
and scatter seeds of birds
across the sky.

It crowbars the senses —
that same sweet pain
of the nail pried
clean of the wood —
that same undoing.

Life moves into the hinges
of things: grape vine,
bean plant, morning glory —
bringing the green world close
as the sky moves farther away.

The old, old story.
The world takes root in the eye.

UFO

Something moves slowly overhead.
The fields fall silent.

Not like a bat, that razors
the face of the moon
and swoops to devour
glinting whiskers;

not like any bird or plane;
not like a deer leaping,
the wind running its comb's teeth
shoulder to flank . . . .

This is a slow turning,
a crackle of colored air
that blots out squares of stars
and swallows Scorpio.

It drags a dark shadow;
the ground goes cold.

It glides out over the lake,
that mirror of dreams
the heart drains into.
Then, it disappears.

Everything comes alive!
crickets, coyotes,
peepers, call out in frenzy:
"See it? See it? See it?"

Yes! I wanted to run!
Instead, I stand here
paralyzed by fear.
That, and loneliness.

Believing in Magic

This hour, washed by blue light!
A rain so soft it has no sound.
Every minute narrows the distance
between our separate days.

You will come home and turn
your key in the lock.
Who will you find
sitting here in my chair?

Streetlights blink on!
Rain on the window glistens —
a forest of stars.
Anything could happen!

Farther Out

Farther out, the ground
drops off and you begin to tread
water in air. The sun
rolls over like a lover
to breathe on your bare shoulder.
Your legs quiver.

Farther out, the earth
falls away and you rise like a
feathered cloud and drift eastward —
the rivers like string; the trees
like silent implosions, so green,
you cannot remember your name.

Farther out, the birds
grow calm and fly with you,
their small *whir whir*
finding a home in your ear.
If you turned around now,
you could greet yourself,
calmly, without any fear.

New Poems

2020 Burning

a covid poem

It's wildfire season.

Unattended sparks are catching in every corner —
smoldering,
seething,
raging into flame;

lifted by winds
to the tops of trees, a fiery crown,
anointing and destroying
everything.

Tiny pathogens catch and spread,
leaping from cell to cell,
devouring the air,
scorching tissues and vessels,
consuming the soft web of the lungs
and the feisty muscles of the heart;
burning down the house

then moving on.

Whole communities are pinned down —
knees on necks —
as they suffer, smolder, and ignite.

My eyes burn hot;
my bangs, my eyelashes
drift away like ashes.

I'm tempted to turn away —
to close my eyes,
cover my ears against
that hot roar,

abandon hope,
evacuate,
flee with my outsized fear
and my paltry possessions.

                and yet . . .
                      and yet . . .

somewhere, small animals
are limping out of the trees.

Somewhere there is a pail of cool water,
a seed of hope,
the balm of kindness.

I need to stop.
Breathe.

I need to turn around
and face the blaze.

Intention

a covid poem

Like everything else these days,
intention is quarantined, hiding,
lost in a cold house
with shades drawn, lights off,
and silence filling the rooms like water.

Outside, the virus is stalking,
leaving footprints in bright snow,
leaving nose prints on the windows,
prying at every cranny
for a way in.

The glow of my computer
brings bad news in waves,
another death every minute,
dozens lost every hour,
thousands more sickened,
struggling to breathe,
struggling to climb out
of that blue wave
then drowning.

Drowning.

Later, intention sits in an upstairs office,
with yellow lamplight pooling in the blue.
As darkness falls, I see its face in the window,
rising out of dark waters,
watching me.

High Wind Warning

The pine trees are swaying
in Pentecostal ecstasy,
heads nodding, eyes closed,
feathery arms reaching up,
in supplication, or prayer.

Snow blows past my window —
glittering midges rising up,
spiraling in a cyclone of light and new life,
and outside, in the locust tree,
an abandoned birdhouse swings wildly,
tossed in the hurricane gale.

I think of bushtits,
lined up like pearls,
huddled deep in the pines —
the fox, curled up in its den,
dreaming of grasshoppers —
and the owl, hunkered down,
unblinking, twisting its head,
listening
for anything other than wind
and its own blind hunger.

Wind knocks at my window.
Fingers pry at the corners.
Outside, everything is howling.
Inside, I sit here
hungry, head tilted
listening for Spring.

Caving

I am well past the middle of this adventure.

When I first dropped in,
I was ill-equipped, endlessly curious,
ready to go anywhere, even
deeper into the dark.

I have bumped along now
for miles, for hours —
passing through narrow corridors,
great, glittering caverns that open up
to blind insects climbing the walls,
water dripping like bells,
and hundreds of soft furred animals
breathing into the dark.

Along the way, I have added protection:
skepticism, wariness —
a growing longing for the light.

If I've made progress in this journey,
It's this:

I am less assured

. . . less certain that I know anything
of this magical path,
this deepening mystery . . .

    . . . more careful to pay attention
     to the growing darkness
     and the vanishing distance . . .

        . . . less sure that it will open up
         to light and grace at the end . . .

>. . . and more urgent in my quest
> to have it *mean* something —
> this journey —

while there is still time
while I still can.

Vigil
For Wendy

We wait, in silence,
for news, for revelation,
for the gathering dark,
and the glittering stars,
blown like frozen tears.

While we wait, we soldier on —
strip the turkey carcass,
toss in carrots and celery;
season with pepper and salt.

We listen to Christmas carols;
put out decorations —
so beloved —
so full of the warmth of history
and the memory of those
who passed them down —

who've now passed on.

We wait
in anguish,
in anticipation,
offering every whispered prayer
to ease the journey,
and unlock the mystery —

focusing on the horizon
where the first sliver of light
will break through,
bringing trees into focus,
birds to their voices
and houses up out of the darkness

bringing the ache of loss
and the promise of life
into the new day.

Grandchild

Once, you were smaller than my thumb —
a mess of cells; a pulp
around a singing seed.

I have seen it grow in you —
how it climbed the keyboard
of your spine and settled
in the space behind your heart.

It will take on a life of its own.
It will call out your hidden names.
Like any bird, its song
will deepen your silences; your dreams will breathe
with the small sound of its sleep.

It will try to fly away —
it will push against the stricture
of your ribs; it will always be pushing.
It will take you away from everything you
have known
and bring you back to a new and
unfamiliar place,
and it will do this
over and over.

When you grow tired, listen . . . .
I will be out here, singing
this hymn of praise,
this lullaby of love.

Late April

At night, the wind goes warming its hands
before it slips in under my hair.
Twilight wanders into the yard.
In the foothills, tiny lights flare up
quick as matchheads.

All day long, robins gathered in the trees,
grasshoppers fled, clacking, over the grass,
and a blue heron sailed effortlessly overhead,
its shadow scrambling over cattails below.

Night floods the patio.
The stars open their eyes, gazing
At the open-mouthed astonishment of moon.
I lie here in silence.

I am as simple,
as insignificant
as waffled blossoms
breathing in the trees
amazed at how sweetly, how easily
they come undone.

What to do with this unfolding —
This extravagance?
                        The wind.
The wind has no answers. It slips in
under my hair, stroking the tiny hairs
that climb up the back of my neck.
Teasing. Promising nothing.

Leaving

Let me leave as the animals do:
softly,
silently,
melting into the trees.

Like the lumbering bear
blending into the bushes —
the white flag of the deer,
flashing surrender —
or the red brush of the fox,
retreating, then extinguished . . .
let me vanish peacefully
into the deep green of evening.

Let the forest close over me
and sleep settle me
as these old bones come undone.

Let my spirit break free,
effervescing like champagne,
pricking the night air
and infusing the world
with gratitude and grace.

Let me leave no trace,
only a rising spark
kindling the day's first light
and joining the raucous birds
in rapture,
in thanksgiving.

To Be Set Adrift....

To be set adrift like a star
in that great wash they call the Milky Way.

This is what you asked for:
to drink wind

where the measure
is too large to be counted,

where bodies of light
seldom collide.

So, dance!
Dance in that vast corridor of silence.

See how the old earth shines
so small and so far away.

About the Author

Rebecca Winning grew up in Springfield, Illinois. She received a BA in English from DePauw University in 1974, attended creative writing classes at Sangamon State University, and received an MA in Creative Writing from the University of Denver in 1979. Her book, *A Cure for Backache and Other Poems* was published in the Sangamon Poets series in 1977; a second book, *A Marriage Pact and Other Poems* was published by Moonsquilt Press in 1983. In 1984, she was selected to participate in the Artists in Education Program, sponsored by the Illinois Council on the Arts and Humanities. Her work, including poetry and short stories, has appeared in a number of literary journals and received numerous awards. For thirty years, she worked in large corporations doing Investor Relations; for the last ten years of her career, she did Community Engagement and Strategy for Jefferson County Public Library. Now retired, she lives in Littleton, Colorado with her husband Jack, with whom she shares two daughters, Shelli and Melissa; a son-in-law, Scott; and four grandchildren, Matthew, Archer, Holland and Walker. She is finally able to devote more time to her writing. Learn more at RebeccaWinningWriter.wordpress.com.

"Publishing books people love reading."
Pearn and Associates, Inc.

<u>Burning Daylight</u> (imprint)

Ikaria, a Love Odyssey on a Greek Island, Anita Sullivan.
Black 14, Ryan Thorburn.
I Look Around for my Life, John Knoepfle.
Cowboy Up, Ryan Thorburn.
It Started & Ended, Bud Grounds.
Lost Cowboys, Ryan Thorburn.
The Bridge of Isfahan, Nilla Cram Cook.
Ever After, Anita Sullivan.
The Border War, Ryan Thorburn.
Men of the Inland Rivers, John Knoepfle.
Swinging Away a Celebration, Victor Pearn.
Adventures of a Footloose Hippie, George M. Eberhart.

<u>Indian Paintbrush Poets</u> (imprint)

Walking in Snow, John Knoepfle.
Then She Kissed El Paco's Lips or April in Dekalb,
    Ricardo Mario Amezquita.
Shadows and Starlight, John Knoepfle.
The Aloe of Evening, John Knoepfle.
Mad Blood, Jim Keller and Murray Moulding, Editors.
Apricot Harvest, Victor Pearn.
Lullaby of Love, Rebecca Winning.
Essay on Air, Victor Pearn.

www.ingramcontent.com/pod-product-compliance
Lightning Source LLC
Chambersburg PA
CBHW052215240426
43670CB00037B/633